THE MESSENGER 2

THE MESSENGER 2

DAPHANNY C. BAKER

Published by J Merrill Publishing, Inc.
2323 W 5th Ave., Suite 120
Columbus, OH 43204
www.JMerrill.pub

Paperback ISBN-13: 978-1-961475-61-8
eBook ISBN-13: 978-1-961475-62-5

Book Title: The Messenger 2
Author: Daphanny C. Baker

Printed in the United States of America
[First Edition]

Sometimes a book is bigger than its author. Maybe, just maybe, it's about the journey—and the people who walk it with you.

I dedicate this book to Tammy Wilson, a friend who has journeyed with me for what "seems like" my entire life. You are, without question, my chosen family. Your friendship has been a beacon of love and "The light." You know my secrets, and I'm certain you've inspired more than a few of them.

I am deeply grateful for the countless times you've served as God's messenger—taking on the sometimes difficult responsibility of delivering His voice to me. Your willingness to obey has helped shape me in ways only God could orchestrate.

You are, truly, the one God gave to me.

FROM THE AUTHOR

Writing is everything to me. It's an outlet to release the dopamine that transcends from a spiritual intellect—one meant to be imparted to God's people. Also, writing is like the flow of breathing for me; it's a must. In this life, one must find their inner peace, which allows you to exhale. This platform allows me to release, scream, cry, and express myself in a manner that others can truly relate to. As you take the time to peruse these pages, allow yourself to be inspired and encouraged to prevail.

CHAPTER 1
LOVE HAS EVERYTHING
TO DO WITH IT!

Should I come to you with a rod, or with love and in the
spirit of meekness?

— I CORINTHIANS 4:21

Anyone can fight. But it takes a determined somebody to love through adversity. As saints, we're often quick to jump on the defensive—ready to get smart, our foreheads crinkling up in a heartbeat. Always reacting: "WHAT?! What'd she say?" "Who is he talking to?" "What was said?!"

Always looking for a battle!

But Deuteronomy 32:35 says, *Vengeance is Mine, and recompense; their foot shall slip in due time; for the day of their calamity is at hand, and the things to come hasten upon them.*

And verse 36 continues: *For the Lord will judge His people and have compassion on His servants, when He sees that their power is gone and there is no one remaining, bond or free.*

I love how my friend Jan handles things—she doesn't have to have the last word. I'm working on that! Trust me, it gets hard, but if it's the last thing I do, I'm going to conquer that urge. Still, I know I can't do it on my own. The problem is (as my husband says), we want to do it in our own strength, in our own timing, but we must follow the leading of the Lord.

Christ said, "If you love me, keep my commandments." (John 14:15)

He goes on: *And I will pray the Father, and He shall give you another Comforter, that He may abide with you forever.*

He will not leave us comfortless! It seems hard, but God's got you —He is right there, leading and guiding you the way you should go.

YOUR RESPONSE NEEDS TO BE DIFFERENT!

The Bible says, *With love and kindness have I drawn thee.* You can't draw anybody by being mean!

And another thing: these days, no one wants to apologize. The world has watered down the apology system—now it's "don't say 'I'm sorry,' say 'I apologize' because you're not sorry." If you have to find a fancy way to apologize to me, you don't mean it! Stop watering down the apology and just say, "I'm sorry."

Love... Love... Love.

Paul was telling the church: "Stop doing these things," but he wrote to them in love. He was careful in his approach.

In everything, it's all in the approach.

As a leader—whether in church or the workplace—I can't just walk up to people with a stern tone and say, "WHAT ARE YOU DOING?" or "Where have you been?" or their Spidey senses go up. They'll immediately go on the defensive.

If someone loves you, they should trust that you're coming from a place of love—a place where your desire is to see them prosper and do right, even if it takes correction. The rod or with love...

Hebrews 12:6 says, *For the Lord disciplines the one He loves, and He chastises every son He receives.*

John 3:16: *For God so loved the world, that He gave His only begotten Son, that whosoever believeth in Him should not perish, but have everlasting life.*

Romans 5:8: *But God commendeth His love toward us, in that, while we were yet sinners, Christ died for us.*

Commendeth means: He demonstrated it!

WHAT'S LOVE GOT TO DO WITH IT? EVERYTHING!

I don't know anyone who would give up their only son. I have two sons, and that seems like an impossible task! There was a time when your word was all people needed. Now, they want you to prove it. Well—God proved what it means to love.

God has given us all the tools we need to live right. He laid the foundation—there are no excuses! We must start being love-minded, not world-minded. We don't want to do things the world's way, but God's way.

Colossians 3:14: *And over all these virtues put on love, which binds them all together in perfect unity.*

I often hear, "Bind us together with cords of love that cannot be broken," but we're so busy stepping on the cord, pulling the cord, or trying to buy our own cord! You can't afford another cord!

1 Corinthians 6:20: *For ye are bought with a price: therefore glorify God in your body, and in your spirit, which are God's.*

You are not your own! So don't treat your life like it belongs to you.

1 John 4:19: *We love because He first loved us.*

Love is love. Christ gave the example—not that "I love you, but I don't like you" business. You may not like the sin I'm in, or what I said, or how I'm acting, but if you genuinely love me, you like me. In marriage, your spouse may get on your last nerve sometimes, but you don't stop loving them. In life, we need a great deal of longsuffering. Jeremiah in the Bible exemplified that trait—showing how believers should respond to challenges and suffering.

Ephesians 4:2: *With all lowliness and gentleness, with longsuffering, bearing with one another in love.*

Romans 5:6: *For when we were yet without strength, in due time Christ died for the ungodly.*

Christ's death is the ultimate demonstration of God's love—love shown even when we were still sinning.

Who wouldn't serve a God who saw us as worthy despite our transgressions? Even though we were lost and undeserving, Jesus paid the price for us.

Revelation 3:15: *I know your works, that you are neither cold nor hot. I could wish you were cold or hot.*

Verse 16: *So then, because you are lukewarm, and neither cold nor hot, I will vomit you out of My mouth.*

It's saying: Make up your mind! For God I'll live, and for God I'll die. Greater is He that is in me than he that is in the world. I am more than a conqueror—not just a conqueror, but more than a conqueror!

1 Peter 4:8: *And above all things have fervent charity among yourselves: for charity shall cover the multitude of sins.*

1 Corinthians 13:4: *Love is patient, love is kind. It does not envy, it does not boast, it is not proud.*

In Hosea 3:1, God tells Hosea to love his wife, Gomer, despite her unfaithfulness—just as God loves Israel despite their idolatry. That's divine restoration and forgiveness.

God asks us for no more than He's already given us. He made the ultimate sacrifice.

WHAT'S LOVE GOT TO DO WITH IT? EVERYTHING!

CHAPTER 2
GOD, HELP ME TO
UNDERSTAND "THIS!"

> 23 *Jesus said to him, "If you can believe, all things are*
> *possible to him who believes."*
> 24 *Immediately the father of the child cried out and said*
> *with tears, "Lord, I believe; help my unbelief!"*
> 25 *When Jesus saw that the people came running together,*
> *He rebuked the unclean spirit, saying to it, "Deaf and*
> *dumb spirit, I command you, come out of him and enter*
> *him no more!"*

> — MARK 9:23–25

This passage captures the desperate prayer of a father who brings his demon-possessed son to Jesus. When the father pleads for help, Jesus responds, "All things are possible for the one who believes." Overwhelmed by both belief and doubt, the father cries out, "I believe; help my unbelief!"—admitting his faith and his struggle at the same time. This honest prayer has become a lifeline for so many believers, a reminder that we can ask God to strengthen our faith when we're wavering.

This is why we must read the Bible—why God left us this book of instructions to help us in trying times. You can't make it without the Word. The stories of the woman with the issue of blood, Daniel in the lion's den, and so many others remind us: sometimes you just don't understand, but you have to hang in there and let God lead and direct you.

Stop trying to do things on your own! You won't make it without Him and His direction.

And YES, we ALL struggle. Sometimes you have to say, "Lord, help my unbelief!" That's real faith—faith that admits the struggle.

You might say, "God, I trust you, but I can't see you."

"God, I trust you, but I can't trace you."

"God, I trust you, but this is uncomfortable for me."

That's when you have to declare the 23rd Psalm: *Yea, though I walk through the valley of the shadow of death, I will fear no evil: for thou art with me; thy rod and thy staff they comfort me. Thou preparest a table before me in the presence of mine enemies: thou anointest my head with oil; my cup runneth over. Surely goodness and mercy shall follow me all the days of my life: and I will dwell in the house of the LORD forever.*

Not just when things look good—forever.

Faith is a journey with ups and downs. It's not all-or-nothing. The father in Mark 9 shows us what it's like to be honest with God—to say, "God, I need your help understanding THIS! This is my child!"

When my own son was sentenced to 6½ to 13 years, I would've lost it if I didn't believe—if I didn't know that God was a keeper and a comforter, I would have lost hope.

Hebrews 11:6 says, *But without faith it is impossible to please Him, for he who comes to God must believe that He is, and that He is a rewarder of those who diligently seek Him.*

Even with imperfect faith, we can approach God. We don't have to know everything or be flawless—but we DO need His help. As Christians, we can tell God about our doubts as well as our beliefs. He already knows anyway!

Have you ever been there?

You read the scriptures, go to church, hear the messages, and you know what God can do—but when it's your situation, you say, "God, help my unbelief."

Help what I can't see. Help me when it's MY situation! I can minister to others, but Lord, help me. I can tell others it will all work out, but when it's my child on death's bed—what do I do now? How do I hold it together as a saint of God? As a First Lady? How do I not fall apart?

Philippians 4:7 (NIV): *And the peace of God, which transcends all understanding, will guard your hearts and your minds in Christ Jesus.*

The New Living Translation says: *Then you will experience God's peace, which exceeds anything we can understand. His peace will guard your hearts and minds as you live in Christ Jesus.

Listen, whatever you need help understanding today—the struggles, the heartaches, the pain—God can help you!

Scripture assures us that even in the most difficult or confusing times, we can experience a divine peace that surpasses our understanding and shields us from anxiety and worry.

Isaiah 26:3 (The Message) says:

"People with their minds set on you, you keep completely whole, steady on their feet, because they keep at it and don't quit."

God, I don't understand this! But I'm not gon' quit.

I can't even fathom what's going on in my life right now... but I'm not gon' quit.

My money is funny.

My change is strange.

My refrigerator is bare.

My car just broke down.

I don't understand THIS! But—I'M NOT GON' QUIT!

If I can just lift mine eyes unto the hills from whence cometh my help.

My help cometh from the Lord, which made heaven and earth. (Psalm 121:1-2)

Keep your eyes on Him. Keep your eyes on the prize, no matter what it looks like. Stay the course!

Isaiah 55:8-9 reminds us:

"For my thoughts are not your thoughts, neither are your ways my ways, saith the LORD. For as the heavens are higher than the earth, so are my ways higher than your ways, and my thoughts than your thoughts."

Thank God He thinks differently than we do. Imagine if God's perspective was as limited as ours! Thank God His view is higher, His plans are better, and His wisdom is beyond anything we could ever imagine.

Job 23:10 says, *"But he knoweth the path that I take: when he hath tried me, I shall come forth as pure gold."*

Proverbs 3:5-6: *Trust in the Lord with all thine heart; and lean not unto thine own understanding. In all thy ways acknowledge him, and he shall direct thy paths.*

You've got to acknowledge Him, and you've sho-nuff got to trust Him.

There's an old song that says, "You will understand it better by and by."

You may not understand the path, but God does. Let Him lead you. Let Him order your steps. He's building your faith.

I Peter 5:10 promises:

But may the God of all grace, who called us to His eternal glory by Christ Jesus, after you have suffered a while, perfect, establish, strengthen, and settle you.

You might think you can't make it.

You might think you're not strong enough.

Wait until God gets through with you!

But you've got to go through the trials.

Even when you don't understand, you've got to stay in the race.

You can't give up.

You can't throw in the towel.

Romans 8:18 says:

For I consider that the sufferings of this present time are not worthy to be compared with the glory which shall be revealed in us.

You will be that preacher.

You will be that missionary.

You will be that prayer warrior.

But you've got to let God do it!

And you've got to stand firm.

Ephesians 4:1—Apostle Paul says:

I, therefore, the prisoner of the Lord, beseech you that ye walk worthy of the vocation wherewith ye are called.

We've got to be found trusting Him.

We've got to be found keeping His commandments.

Walking worthy of the call.

Keep your relationship with Him intact.

Thank Him every day for the sacrifice He made for us.

CHAPTER 3

DON'T LET
NOTHING STOP YOU!

Esther 4:11–17

Esther's story is one of courage and divine purpose. When the king's official, Haman, plotted to destroy the Jews, Esther—a young woman living in captivity—was positioned by God to make a difference. She risked her life to approach the king, knowing the law forbade anyone, even the queen, from coming uninvited. But with her people's lives at stake, she declared, "If I perish, I perish."

Let me give you a little background:

Esther was born during Israel's captivity, a consequence of their disobedience to God. She rose from obscurity to become queen and, when her people were threatened, she chose faith over fear. Mordecai, her cousin, reminded her: "Who knows but that you have come to your royal position for such a time as this?"

Esther's story calls us to model our lives after her bravery, devotion, and tenacity.

Romans 8:38–39 reminds us:

> *For I am convinced that neither death nor life, neither*
> *angels nor demons, neither the present nor the future,*

> *nor any powers, neither height nor depth, nor anything*
> *else in all creation, will be able to separate us from the*
> *love of God that is in Christ Jesus our Lord.*

Esther called the people to fast for three days—no eating or drinking, just seeking God's face. She denied herself, turned it over to God, and moved forward in faith. That's determination. That's surrender.

YOU MUST BE DETERMINED, JUST LIKE ESTHER, TO TAKE A STAND NO MATTER WHAT!

No matter what it looks like, no matter how it feels, no matter what anyone says, and no matter what power anyone else seems to have.

Psalm 118:6 says, *The Lord is on my side; I will not fear. What can man do unto me?*

Esther was so determined, she was prepared to die for the cause. That's how we should be—standing up for Christ, unwavering, undeterred! "I will go, even if I have to go by myself!"

Philippians 4:13 says, *I can do all things through Christ who strengthens me.*

All things! This is light work when God is on your side. To be honest, all you need is God. *Greater is He that is in me than he that is in the world!* (1 John 4:4)

Cooks say, "Add a little flavor and it's edible." I say, add a whole lot of Jesus and it's doable!

Philippians 4:6–7:

> *Be careful for nothing; but in everything by prayer and*
> *supplication with thanksgiving let your requests be*
> *made known unto God. And the peace of God, which*
> *passeth all understanding, shall keep your hearts and*
> *minds through Christ Jesus.*

Esther's fast was powerful. Fasting is essential. It adds tenacity you didn't know you had. You'll find yourself walking around declaring, "I'm victorious! I'm more than a conqueror!"

When the situation seems too big for you, it's just the right size for God.

Ephesians 2:10:

For we are God's handiwork, created in Christ Jesus to do good works, which God prepared in advance for us to do.

You need God to anoint your works! Some of our work is weak— let God strengthen it.

James 2:14–17:

> *What does it profit, my brethren, if someone says he has*
> *faith but does not have works? ... Thus also faith by*
> *itself, if it does not have works, is dead.*

Let Esther's actions give you the confidence to embrace your destiny, use your influence for good, and leave a legacy of bravery and faith. She was willing to risk her life for God's plan. Strategically positioned, Esther shows us that God can use anyone—no matter your background or skill set. If you let Him, God can use your life for His glory!

Jeremiah 29:11 (NIV):

> *"For I know the plans I have for you," declares the Lord,*
> *"plans to prosper you and not to harm you, plans to*
> *give you hope and a future."*

Don't let anything stop you! Stand up, step out, and trust God to do the impossible.

CHAPTER 4
I AM BUILT FOR IT

> 24 Therefore whosoever heareth these sayings of mine, and
> doeth them, I will liken him unto a wise man, which
> built his house upon a rock:
> 25 And the rain descended, and the floods came, and the
> winds blew, and beat upon that house; and it fell not:
> for it was founded upon a rock.

> — MATTHEW 7:24–25

Can you imagine a tornado coming through, but your house, your family, your things—left untouched?

To be built to stand means something was designed and constructed to last. Someone took time and care to make sure it would endure—relevant, strong, and valuable. Endurance is the aim: not just looking good for a moment, but surviving the test of time. That's what God is calling us to—steadfast, unmovable, ALWAYS abounding in the work of the Lord!

Let nothing move you. Always give yourselves fully to the

> *work of the Lord, because you know that your labor in
> the Lord is not in vain.*

— 1 CORINTHIANS 15:58 (NIV)

Think about those old cars—solid steel, hard to dent. Today's cars? A shopping cart can do damage! God wants us to be like those classics—built to last, not flimsy or easily shaken.

> *Remember, there is only one foundation, the one already
> laid: Jesus Christ. Take particular care in picking out
> your building materials. Eventually there is going to be
> an inspection.*

— 1 CORINTHIANS 3:11–12 (MSG)

Jesus uses the parable of the wise and foolish builders to drive home the point: hearing His words isn't enough. You have to do them, live them, build on them. If you do, you'll stand through the storms. If you don't, you'll crumble when trouble comes.

The enemy knows what God put in you. That's why he tries to convince you that you can't make it, that it's too hard, that you should give up. He can see your potential, even when you don't. That's why he keeps coming after you—he doesn't want you quoting, "I can do all things through Christ who strengthens me" (Phil 4:13), or "Greater is He that is in me than he that is in the world" (1 John 4:4), or "I'm more than a conqueror" (Rom 8:37).

If you know who you are, you'll keep encouraging yourself with scripture:

- *When the enemy comes in like a flood, the Spirit of the Lord
  will lift up a standard against him (Isa 59:19).*
- *Though I walk through the valley of the shadow of death, I will
  fear no evil, for you are with me (Psalm 23:4–5).*

You were built for it.
Built to overcome.
Built to make a difference.
Built to be someone—not just anybody, but a world-changer.
You were built to weather the storm, no matter what it is!
Listening to Jesus isn't enough—you have to live out His Word. Wisdom is applying what you know so you can withstand life's trials.

My son, if sinners entice you, don't be persuaded.

— PROVERBS 1:10

Don't let temptation shake your foundation.

*The eyes of the LORD are in every place, beholding the evil
    and the good.*

— PROVERBS 15:3

God sees you. Don't let your flesh make your foundation shaky or cause all you've built to be weakened. Keep going, stay in the race, and seek God's face often.

*But without faith it is impossible to please Him: for he that
    cometh to God must believe that He is, and that He is a
    rewarder of them that diligently seek Him.*

— HEBREWS 11:6

Be diligent in your building—don't come off the wall, no matter what!
No matter the circumstance, no matter what others are doing, stand strong.

> *Be strong in the Lord, and in the power of His might. Put on*
> *the whole armor of God, that you may be able to stand*
> *against the wiles of the devil.*

— EPHESIANS 6:10–11

The devil wants to sift you, but you've got to stand your ground—ten toes down, standing on business.

And do it phenomenally!

As Maya Angelou said, "I'm a woman. Phenomenally."

Let your inner power and grace shine—not from outward show, but from what God has built in you.

While others are being seductive, you build a life of good character. While they're at the club, you're at revival. While they're cussing, you're showing grace. Don't be the one who always has to "get somebody together"—let God handle that. He's coming back for a church without spot or wrinkle (Eph 5:27). Vengeance is His, not yours (Rom 12:19).

> *The thief comes only to steal, kill, and destroy; I have come*
> *that they might have life, and have it more abundantly.*

— JOHN 10:10

The foundation is already laid—just build on it!

> *Build up yourselves on your most holy faith, praying in the*
> *Holy Ghost.*

— JUDE 1:20

Keep strengthening your faith. Stay in God's love. Pray in the Spirit.

Make your declaration:

"God, I need you. God, I can't do this without you. There is none like you. I can search through eternity and I'll find there is no one like you!"

CHAPTER 5
THE ALTAR IS WHAT ALTERS YOUR LIFE

Is anyone among you suffering? He must pray. Is anyone joyful? He is to sing praises [to God]. Is anyone among you sick? He must call for the elders (spiritual leaders) of the church and they are to pray over him, anointing him with oil in the name of the Lord; and the prayer of faith will restore the one who is sick, and the Lord will raise him up; and if he has committed sins, he will be forgiven. Therefore, confess your sins to one another [your false steps, your offenses], and pray for one another, that you may be healed and restored. The heartfelt and persistent prayer of a righteous man (believer) is able to accomplish much [when put into action and made effective by God—it is dynamic and can have tremendous power].

— JAMES 5:13–18 (AMP)

In the Bible, prayer isn't about a set number of times—it's about a lifestyle, a constant connection with God. Daniel and David prayed morning, noon, and night, but the New Testament tells us to pray "constantly." The altar—whether it's at church, in your car, your kitchen, or your bedroom—is a sacred place where you meet God, lay down your burdens, and let Him work on you. Some want God to alter their lives without ever visiting the altar. You can't have one without the other!

Pray without ceasing.

— I

THESSALONIANS 5:17

Unceasing prayer is more than words—it's an ongoing conversation, a mindset, a way of living where prayer is always your first response. When I started out, I wanted God to bless my children, make a way, keep me safe, but I had no real prayer life! I remember in Germany, when Mother Robinson put me on the program to pray. I told her, "I don't pray in public!" She said, "I'm going to keep putting you on, because prayer is what will keep you when times get hard." I didn't get mad—I adjusted my prayer life. I prayed more privately, so I wouldn't be embarrassed publicly!

WHAT DOES YOUR PRAYER LIFE LOOK LIKE AT HOME?

You can't keep asking God for things with no relationship. The altar is where you build that relationship. It's where you offer yourself, where you get real with God. Your altar can be anywhere—just don't leave home without it! It's what keeps you grounded, focused, and steady throughout the day.

WHY IS THE ALTAR SO IMPORTANT?

- It's where you present your sacrifice, acknowledging God's presence—even when you don't feel it.

- Your posture in prayer reveals the state of your spiritual life.

Let me be real:
    If you're falling out every five minutes,
    If you're always ready to give up,
    If anything can ruffle your feathers—
    You're not praying!
    You're not trusting God to handle it!
    You're not taking your burdens to the Lord and leaving them there!

> *Be anxious for nothing, but in everything by prayer and supplication, with thanksgiving, let your requests be made known to God; and the peace of God, which surpasses all understanding, will guard your hearts and minds through Christ Jesus.*
>
> *— PHILIPPIANS 4:6–7*

You'll be at peace—no matter what it looks like!

> *And my God shall supply all your needs according to His riches in glory.*
>
> *— PHILIPPIANS 4:19*

Prayer is like having a mic that never turns off—God hears you, even when you whisper, "God, I can't do this without you. God, this is bigger than me!"

> *Looking unto Jesus the author and finisher of our faith; who for the joy set before Him endured the cross...*
>
> *— HEBREWS 12:2*

He's the example—He went through suffering and came out victorious. You can too, but you have to pray! Keep an altar on site, in your purse, in your heart. It's your weapon, your anchor, your sanity.

> *If you believe, you will receive whatever you ask for in prayer.*
>
> — MATTHEW 21:22

Put your hand on your chest and say: IN PRAYER!
You can't do any of this without it.

> *The effectual fervent prayer of a righteous man avails much!*
>
> — JAMES 5:16B

The altar anchors you.
The altar assures you.
The altar keeps you grounded and on the right path.
The altar causes things to shift around you.
When you put things on the altar, God can do what He pleases with them. Sometimes all you can say is "HELP!"—and God is obligated to respond. When you recognize your limitation, God shows up with His manifestation.
I'm limited—but with God, it's endless!

> *I can do all things through Christ who strengthens me.*
>
> — PHILIPPIANS 4:13

*The Spirit helps us in our weakness. We do not know what
we ought to pray for, but the Spirit Himself intercedes
for us through wordless groans.*

— ROMANS 8:26

Sometimes the Spirit will pray for you in ways you can't even express. Let God take it from here. You can't do any of this without a prayer life—without the altar.

Jessica Reedy wrote, "Put it on the altar—everything you've been worried about, put it on the altar."

Nolan Williams Jr. wrote, "Take it to the Lord in prayer."

CHAPTER 6
GOD IS IN THE MIDST OF IT!!

Astonished, King Nebuchadnezzar stood up in terror, and
asked his advisors, "Didn't we throw three men into the
fire, bound firmly with ropes?"
"Yes, your majesty."
"Look!" he told them, "I see four men walking untied and
unharmed in the middle of the fire, and the appearance
of the fourth resembles a divine being."

— DANIEL 3:24–25

Do you ever feel like you're in this fight all alone? Like you have absolutely no one—friends and acquaintances have turned their backs, you can't even buy a friend, and it feels like you're wandering the wilderness solo?

I came to tell "us" that—even in the midst of it—God is right there. When it seems all hope is lost, He steps in and shows Himself mightily.

I say "us" because I get it! There was a time when I felt this way—alone, with only my children, and even they were busy at times. Every time I thought I could trust someone, God would quickly show me that relationship wasn't in alignment with my journey. I said, "Okay God, what is this about?" I finally said, "Well, I'm done trying to have a friend!" And just at that moment of relinquishment, God sent someone to walk beside me in ministry, to hold my arms up. You may THINK you're alone, but God said He will never leave you nor forsake you! (Hebrews 13:5)

You may feel like you're walking alone, but remember:

Yea, though I walk through the valley of the shadow of death, I will fear no evil, for Thou art with me.

He's with me when I come in, He's with me when I go out, He's with me on my job, He's with me even when I can't feel Him! Even when it looks like "this has got to be the devil," God is still right there. Sometimes He may not have orchestrated the trouble, but He's still present. Sometimes, He DOES orchestrate it—just like with Job.

> *The LORD said to Satan, "Have you considered My servant Job? For there is no one like him on the earth, a blameless and upright man, fearing God and turning away from evil."*
>
> — JOB 1:8

Put your own name there: "Have you considered my servant ______?"

That means God trusts you to keep trusting Him in the midst of it! He'll never let you be thrown into the fire alone—He'll always be right there.

Shadrach, Meshach, and Abednego were thrown into the fiery furnace for their faithfulness, but King Nebuchadnezzar saw a fourth man in the fire—a divine presence.

So next time someone asks, "Is it just you?"—say, "No, it's TWO of us! I'm never alone. Someone always has my back!"

The battle is not yours!

The LORD will fight for you; you need only to be still.

— EXODUS 14:14

You're all worked up for nothing! Losing sleep for nothing. You've got this! The way was already made when He allowed you to go through.

And get this—not everyone is considered. Sometimes we rebuke the very storm God wants us to endure! It didn't come to kill you; it came to give you life. Not for your descending, but for your ascending. God is trying to elevate you, but you're running from your promotion! He knows what you can take and has every situation under control.

You might FEEL alone.

It may SEEM hopeless.

It may LOOK like it's the end.

But God is right there!

Even when it's hard, God is IN you.

Greater is He that is in me than he that is in the world.

— 1 JOHN 4:4

A thousand may fall at your side, ten thousand at your right hand, but it will not come near you.

— PSALM 91:7

Because you have made the Lord your dwelling place—no evil shall befall you.

— PSALM 91:9–10

If God is for us, who can be against us?

— ROMANS 8:31

I've never trusted God more than I do now. Life has made it so we have no choice but to trust Him! The world is changing, love is growing cold, and people fall out with each other like tomorrow is promised. God is watching every action, every deed, every word.

Lo, I am with you always, even to the end of the age.

— MATTHEW 28:20

Ezekiel called Him a "wheel in the middle of a wheel"—God is omnipresent!

He's always present.

All you have to do is ask for His help, trust Him, and lean not on your own understanding. (Proverbs 3:5–6)

All you have to do is have faith:

Now faith is the substance of things hoped for, the evidence of things not seen. (Hebrews 11:1)

But without faith it is impossible to please Him... (Hebrews 11:6)

God is right there in the midst of it!

Trust Him.

Believe in Him.

Seek Him.

So do not fear, for I am with you; do not be dismayed, for I am your God. I will strengthen you and help you; I will uphold you with my righteous right hand.

— ISAIAH 41:10 (NIV)

I sought the LORD, and He answered me and delivered me from all my fears. Those who look to Him are radiant,

*and their faces shall never be ashamed. Oh, taste and
see that the LORD is good! Blessed is the one who takes
refuge in Him!*

— PSALM 34:4–5, 8

Take refuge! Don't let the enemy trick you into thinking God has left you—no matter what you've done, said, or where you've been, or how old you are.

*Be strong and courageous. Do not be frightened, and do not
be dismayed, for the LORD your God is with you
wherever you go.*

— JOSHUA 1:9

When the enemy thinks he's about to trip you up, God is right there.

Late in the midnight hour, when your body is wracked with pain—God is right there.

When you feel alone—God is right there.

Even in the midst of it, God is in the midst of it!

He's your heavy load bearer, your problem solver, your help, your hope, the author and finisher of your faith.

If you need love—He's there.

If you need joy—He's there.

If you need peace—He's there.

He's your beginning and your end.

He's better than any friend—He's your friend till the end.

God is right there in the midst of it!

CHAPTER 7

RELIGIOSITY VS CHRISTIANITY

THERE'S A DIFFERENCE

> *As Jesus and his disciples traveled, they came to a village*
> *where Martha opened her home. While Martha was*
> *busy serving, her sister Mary sat at Jesus' feet, listening.*
> *Martha, frustrated, asked Jesus to tell Mary to help her.*
> *But Jesus replied, "Martha, Martha, you are worried*
> *and upset about many things, but few things are*
> *needed—or indeed only one. Mary has chosen what is*
> *better, and it will not be taken away from her."*
> *Martha was caught up in the busyness of serving, but*
> *Mary chose to be present with Jesus. Jesus gently*
> *corrected Martha, reminding her that the "one thing"*
> *that truly matters is being with Him.*

> — LUKE 10:38–42

Religiosity is a sociological term describing the quality of a person's religious beliefs or devotion—the outward appearance, the routines, the traditions. It's the sense that you have to be busy, always doing something, to prove your commitment.

Christianity, at its core, simply means being "Christ-like."

It's about character, not just activity.

It's about relationship, not just ritual.

You see the difference already?

Religiosity is long-winded—full of rules, explanations, and self-justification.

Christianity is simple: be like Jesus.

This passage reminds us that, while daily responsibilities matter, we must never neglect time at Jesus' feet. Whether through prayer, Bible study, or quiet moments in God's presence, our spiritual connection with Him is essential.

Too often, Christ is left out of our "church work." We get busy for Him, but don't spend time with Him. Jesus repeatedly called out religious leaders—and even His own followers—for getting caught up in cycles of self-glorification and missing the true heart of God.

Matthew 23 tells how Jesus, surrounded by religious authorities flaunting their knowledge and status, says, "They know their stuff, but their hearts are no good."

You might be a good usher, a gifted singer, or a talented leader—but what does your heart look like?

Are you anointed, or just busy?

Did God set His seal on all this "work," or are you missing the point?

There must be balance in the church.

Jeremiah 3:14–15 says God will give us shepherds after His own heart—leaders who feed us with knowledge and understanding, so the ministry functions smoothly and newcomers are welcomed and discipled.

Every member matters.

No one should do all the work, nor should old members guard their positions out of fear. That's religiosity—busy for the wrong reasons.

Romans 2:6–8 reminds us: God will repay each person according to their deeds. Eternal life is for those who persist in doing good for God's glory—not those who serve themselves.

It's not about earthly rewards or recognition.

Nothing here on earth, not even my birthday celebrations, compares to the reward waiting in heaven.

All the glory belongs to God!

Glory belongs to God, whose power is at work in us. By this power He can do infinitely more than we can ask or imagine.

— EPHESIANS 3:20

They did not gain possession of the land by their own sword... but by Your right hand, Your arm, and the light of Your countenance, because You favored them.

— PSALMS 44:3

We can't do anything in our own strength.

God gave us our gifts and abilities—let's use them to build up, not tear down, the ministry.

A few weeks ago, a minister in our church was overwhelmed: children's practice, church cleaning, a family baby shower—all in one day. She asked, "First lady, how will I get all this done?" I told her, "Pray and ask God for guidance."

With strategic planning, she did it all—without neglecting God's work or her personal commitments. Most people would have canceled the church part first!

Why is it that, when life gets busy, the first thing we drop is church?

We have an obligation to God and to our daily lives.

I must work the works of Him who sent me while it is day; night is coming when no one can work.

— JOHN 9:4

Night symbolizes death; time is limited. So live a life pleasing to God while you still have breath.

CHAPTER 8
THE CHOICE IS YOURS

> *Do not turn aside from any of the commands I give you*
> *today, to the right or to the left, following other gods*
> *and serving them. However, if you do not obey the Lord*
> *your God and do not carefully follow all his commands*
> *and decrees I am giving you today, all these curses will*
> *come on you and overtake you.*
>
> — DEUTERONOMY 28:14–15

Choice—it's the act of selecting or deciding between two or more options.

- The choice between good and evil
- The choice between right and wrong
- The choice between holy and unholy
- The choice between faith and fear
- The choice between keeping God's commandments or not

You have a choice!

A bit of context:

In Deuteronomy 28, God promises Israel that if they obey, He'll open the heavens and pour out blessings—they'll be lenders, not borrowers, and rain will fall at just the right time. But if they disobey, curses will follow. The message is clear: obedience brings life and blessing, while disobedience brings consequences. God's commands aren't meant to burden us, but to lead us into purpose and joy.

God knows the path we should take. He knows what's best—we just have to trust and obey Him.

Choice means:

- Alternative
- Election
- Option
- Preference
- Selection

God gives us the privilege of choosing freely. In Genesis, Adam was given a choice: obey or disobey God's command about the tree. That freedom is still ours today. God lays out His commandments, but it's up to us to obey.

You choose to love or not.

You choose to tell the truth or spread lies.

You choose to honor your parents or not.

You choose to avoid envy.

It's your choice!

As Christians, we have the freedom to choose whether we'll sin or honor God.

> *Don't give sin a vote in how you conduct your lives. Don't*
> *even run little errands connected with that old way of*
> *life. Throw yourselves wholeheartedly and full-time*
> *into God's way of doing things!*
>
> — ROMANS 6:12–13 (MSG)

Our desires are real, but we must be sure they don't conflict with God's will.

> *The thief comes only to steal, kill, and destroy; I have come*
> *that they may have life, and have it more abundantly.*
>
> — JOHN 10:10

Temptations will come, but you have the choice to resist. God will never let temptation overpower you.

> *All things are lawful for me, but not all things are*
> *beneficial. All things are lawful, but not everything*
> *builds up.*
>
> — 1 CORINTHIANS 10:23

Don't seek your own way. Don't create your own plan. Don't design your own destiny apart from God. The choice is yours—but choose wisely!

> *Walk in the Spirit, and you will not fulfill the lust of the*
> *flesh.*
>
> — GALATIANS 5:16

Let the Holy Spirit guide your decisions, not your old nature.

> *Do not be conformed to this world, but be transformed by*
> *the renewing of your mind, that you may prove what is*
> *that good, acceptable, and perfect will of God.*
>
> — ROMANS 12:2

Your old mind will say, "Just this once."

Your old mind will say, "No one will know."
Your old mind will say, "Everyone else is doing it!"
But what does God's word say?

Nothing unclean will enter it, nor anyone who does what is
detestable or false, but only those whose names are
written in the Lamb's book of life.

— REVELATION 21:27

I want to hear Him say, "Well done."
I want to make it in.
Nothing compares to what God has for us on the other side.
No sin, no lie, no shortcut is worth missing out on God's promise.
Do not be overcome by evil, but overcome evil with good.
Let your light so shine before men, that they may see your good works
and glorify your Father in heaven.

Choose to be the light.
Choose to live for Christ.
Choose to be saved.
Choose to be different.
Choose to follow peace and righteousness.
Let Him lead and guide you.
Hold on. Stay in the race.
Don't give up. Stay fixed and focused.
Keep your eye on the prize!

CHAPTER 9

I REFUSE TO AID SATAN IN STOPPING ME

> *God asked Satan, "What have you been up to?"*
> *Satan answered, "Oh, going here and there, checking things*
> *out."*
> *God said, "Have you noticed my friend Job? There's no one*
> *quite like him—honest, true, devoted to God, hating*
> *evil. He's still holding on to his integrity! You tried to*
> *trick me into destroying him, but it didn't work."*
> *Satan replied, "A human would do anything to save his life.*
> *But if you reached down and took away his health, he'd*
> *curse you to your face, that's what."*
>
> — JOB 2:2–5 (MSG)

In Job 2, Satan is allowed to test Job's health after failing to break his faith through material loss. Job is covered in sores, suffering deeply, yet he refuses to curse God—even when his wife urges him to give up. Job stands firm, even in agony.

*Submit yourselves therefore to God. Resist the devil, and he
will flee from you.*

— JAMES 4:7

The Bible is clear: resist temptation and depend on God for strength. With God's help, you can overcome even the hardest circumstances!

*Put on the full armor of God, so that you can take your
stand against the devil's schemes.*

— EPHESIANS 6:11

Satan might be after me, but I refuse to help him.

- I may wake up in pain, but I'm not staying home.
- I might get upset with the Pastor or First Lady, but I'm
  going to church and making it right.
- I'm not giving the enemy any help!

When I was nine, a man robbed my uncle and me at gunpoint. I refused to cooperate—I wouldn't lie down, wouldn't reveal where the money was, wouldn't let him cover my mouth. Eventually, he left empty-handed.

DON'T HELP THE DEVIL. DON'T PLAY WITH HIM. DON'T PARTICIPATE IN HIS SCHEMES.

Abstain from all appearance of evil.

— 1 THESSALONIANS 5:22

Stay away from anything that even looks wrong. Run from things that stir up your old desires. Walk in the Spirit, not in the cravings of the flesh.

Do not be overcome by evil, but overcome evil with good.

— ROMANS 12:21

RUN TO THE HOUSE OF GOD!

The enemy wants you to stay home and miss the tools and teaching you need. He wants you to say "woe is me," to focus on your lack, to miss the message that you are more than a conqueror and that God is your provider!

Job stood strong in adversity. He didn't give up. God had faith in Job!

My husband always says, "The thing is, God can't consider some of us because we won't show Him we're credible—we give up too easily!"

Four things you must do:

1. Accept correction.
2. Accept delays—delayed doesn't mean denied.
3. Overcome obstacles—life gets heavy sometimes.
4. Stay in the race.

No matter what it looks or feels like, get some faith and trust God in the middle of it.

Trust in the Lord with all your heart; lean not on your own understanding. In all your ways acknowledge Him, and He will direct your paths.

— PROVERBS 3:5–6

Don't assist the enemy!

- The devil needs your hands to slap someone.
- He needs two people to divorce.
- He needs you to throw in the towel to make you quit.
- He needs your mouth to start an argument.

BRIDLE YOUR TONGUE—LET YOUR WORDS EDIFY.

Sing, "Order my steps in Your word!" (Kirk Franklin)

Get YOU a song—sing hymns and melodies aloud and in your heart.

- It encourages unity.
- Declares faith.
- Fights evil.
- Brings comfort in trials.

Paul and Silas prayed and sang hymns at midnight.
Suddenly, an earthquake shook the prison, the doors
flew open, and everyone's chains came loose.

— ACTS 16:25–26

DON'T FALL INTO THE TRAPS OF THE ENEMY. DON'T PUT YOURSELF IN COMPROMISING POSITIONS.

Put on the Lord Jesus Christ, and make no provision for the
flesh, to gratify its desires.

— ROMANS 13:14

Live a transformed life. Reject the old self. Pursue holiness—nothing should matter more than making it in!

- Not the flesh!
- Not a snapback!
- Not retaliation!
- Nothing!

I won't let anything separate me from the love of Christ. I won't let anything keep me from making it in.

The devil comes to steal, kill, and destroy—but Jesus came that you might have life, and have it more abundantly

— JOHN 10:10

Though He slay me, yet will I trust Him

— JOB 13:15

A thousand may fall at your side, but it will not come near you

— PSALM 91:7

The Lord is my light and my salvation; whom shall I fear?
The Lord is the strength of my life; of whom shall I be
afraid?
When the wicked came against me, they stumbled and fell.
Though an army encamp against me, my heart shall
not fear; though war rise against me, in this I will be
confident.
One thing I have desired of the Lord, that will I seek: that I
may dwell in the house of the Lord all the days of
my life

— PSALM 27:1–4

CHAPTER 10
SIMPLY REDEEMED

> *Therefore, there is now no condemnation for those who are*
> *in Christ Jesus, because through Christ Jesus the law of*
> *the Spirit who gives life has set you free from the law of*
> *sin and death. For what the law was powerless to do*
> *because it was weakened by the flesh, God did by*
> *sending his own Son in the likeness of sinful flesh to be*
> *a sin offering. And so he condemned sin in the flesh, in*
> *order that the righteous requirement of the law might*
> *be fully met in us, who do not live according to the flesh*
> *but according to the Spirit. Those who live according to*
> *the flesh have their minds set on what the flesh desires;*
> *but those who live in accordance with the Spirit have*
> *their minds set on what the Spirit desires.*
>
> — ROMANS 8:1–5

Let's talk about what it really means to be redeemed.

In Genesis 3, Adam and Eve's disobedience brought sin, sorrow, and death into the world. That "Fall" meant every generation since has inherited a fallen nature. But even then, God's love didn't run out—He provided for them, set a boundary, and began a plan of redemption that would ultimately restore our relationship with Him through Jesus Christ.

God could have started over, wiped the slate clean, and created new humans. But He didn't. He didn't throw Adam and Eve away. He doesn't throw us away, either. Even when we fall short, He keeps making a way, keeps opening doors, keeps loving us.

Don't get it twisted—He does discipline us.

> *Because the Lord disciplines the one he loves, and he*
> *chastens everyone he accepts as his son.*

> — HEBREWS 12:6

When you're a child, your parent doesn't send you away when you mess up—they correct you. My adopted mom wasn't even my biological mother, but she made a promise to my mom on her deathbed: she'd raise me right. She'd "get me" right where I showed out, but she never threatened to send me away. She corrected me because she loved me.

WHAT DOES IT MEAN TO BE FORGIVEN?

Forgiveness is at the heart of God's character and a requirement for us as believers.

> *If we confess our sins, he is faithful and just and will*
> *forgive us our sins and purify us from all*
> *unrighteousness.*

> — 1 JOHN 1:9

The Bible is full of forgiveness stories—Joseph forgave his brothers (Genesis 45), David forgave Saul (1 Samuel 24), and Jesus forgave those who crucified Him (Luke 23:34):

"Father, forgive them, for they know not what they do."

Imagine that—praying for the forgiveness of those who are hurting you! Jesus knew Judas would betray Him, but He still broke bread with him.

Christ died to take the place of sin, so we could have a right to the tree of life. But you still have to live right! Forgiveness is a gift, but it's also a responsibility—just like a parent who buys you a car for graduation. If you stop doing your part, you won't get the keys!

WALK WORTHY OF YOUR CALLING.

*I urge you to walk in a manner worthy of the calling to
which you have been called.*

— EPHESIANS 4:1–3

Not "He died and that's it"—we have work to do, too!
Not only does God forgive us, He expects us to forgive others.

*But if you do not forgive others their sins, your Father will
not forgive your sins.*

— MATTHEW 6:15

Forgiveness is the only way to be truly free.

*Looking unto Jesus, the author and finisher of our faith,
who for the joy set before Him endured the cross...*

— HEBREWS 12:2

Jesus is our example—not the world. Through His death, we're set free from condemnation. God doesn't see us as guilty anymore.

But God demonstrates his own love for us in this: While we
were still sinners, Christ died for us.

— ROMANS 5:8

He loved us while we were still sinners.
We're free because He loved us.
We're free because He laid down His life for us.
You may have fallen, but you are forgiven.
Now walk like you're free!

CHAPTER 11
GOD IS A CONSUMING FIRE

The words "once more" indicate the removing of what can be shaken—that is, created things—so that what cannot be shaken may remain. Therefore, since we are receiving a kingdom that cannot be shaken, let us be thankful, and so worship God acceptably with reverence and awe, for our "God is a consuming fire."

— HEBREWS 12:27–29

The Message Bible puts it this way:

God is not an indifferent bystander. He's actively cleaning house, torching all that needs to burn, and He won't quit until it's all cleansed. God Himself is Fire!

Deuteronomy 4:24 is the root of this truth—God's presence is both majestic and severe. His righteousness will ultimately destroy everything that's fleeting and worthless.

You cannot keep acting out of order and expect no consequences. Only what you do for Christ will last.

> *For the wrath of God is being revealed from heaven against*
> *all ungodliness and wickedness of people who suppress*
> *the truth by their wickedness.*

> — ROMANS 1:18

You can't keep living in sin and think you'll get by. God will consume everything in you that's not like Him—so you can become like Him!

And another thing—(as my Bishop in Kentucky would say), when you see others doing wrong, don't get weary or try to fix it yourself.

> *Beloved, never avenge yourselves, but leave it to the wrath*
> *of God, for it is written, "Vengeance is mine, I will*
> *repay, says the Lord."*

> — ROMANS 12:19

God is NOT in a gang! He doesn't need your help to get revenge. He just wants you to live right—He'll take care of the rest.

I'm a Jersey girl, so before I got "real" saved, my mindset was always to protect myself. Sometimes it feels like God is taking too long to handle those who wrong us! But then I remember the grace He's shown me—the mercy He extended when I deserved correction. In the moments I wanted to "get someone together," God could've taken me out, but His grace kept me.

The song says, "Oh for grace to trust You more!"

I trust Him when I can't feel Him.

I trust Him when I can't see Him.

> *Trust in the Lord with all your heart and lean not on your*
> *own understanding; in all your ways acknowledge*
> *Him, and He will direct your paths.*

> — PROVERBS 3:5–6

Some see God's wrath as a remedy for brokenness—a fair reaction to sin. Others see it as an expression of His holiness and love for justice. Either way, His wrath is never random. It's always tied to His love and His desire to see us purified.

Do you realize God could've taken you out a long time ago? But His love gives you another chance—"Come on, daughter! Get it right, son!" He is patient and never abuses His authority.

God is a consuming fire, and at any moment, He could stop us in our tracks. But He is also gracious and merciful—the All-Sufficient One, the "wheel in the middle of a wheel," the "late in the midnight hour God," the "I've got you" type of God!

God is a consuming fire, but He's also a God of grace. Don't take His grace for granted.

> *What shall we say then? Shall we continue in sin so that grace may abound?*
>
> — ROMANS 6:1

In Christian life, "consuming fire" means God destroys what's evil and purifies what's precious. He wants to refine us! Sometimes we get so distracted and preoccupied that He has to "burn up" the junk that blinds us—because His love for us is so strong.

Sometimes you have to clean house to see how beautiful it really is!

Because He loves you, He'll chasten you.

> *For whom the Lord loves, He chastens, and scourges every son whom He receives.*
>
> — HEBREWS 12:6

The Message says, "It's the child He loves that He disciplines; the child He embraces, He also corrects."

Remember when your mom said, "I whooped you because I love

you?" It hurts now, but it saves you from greater pain later. God sometimes has to stop us in our tracks to keep us from a path of no return. The fire isn't meant to destroy you—it's meant to refine you!

Gold isn't authentic until it's been through the fire.

My husband says, "A tea bag isn't good until it's dipped in scalding water!"

The fire isn't for your detriment—it's for your development.

> *But He knows the way that I take; when He has tried me, I shall come forth as gold.*

> — JOB 23:10

> *The enemy wants to see you destroyed, but God came that you might have life—abundant life!*

> — JOHN 10:10

> *Though He slay me, yet will I trust Him*

> — JOB 13:15

> *I will bless the Lord at all times—His praise shall continually be in my mouth!*

> — PSALM 34:1

CHAPTER 12
CHILE', IT DOESN'T GET ANY BETTER THAN THIS

> *"Take this child home and nurse him for me," the princess*
> *instructed the baby's mother, "and I will pay you well!"*
> *So she took him home and nursed him. Later, when he*
> *was older, she brought him back to the princess and he*
> *became her son. She named him Moses (meaning "to*
> *draw out") because she had drawn him out of the*
> *water.*

> — EXODUS 2:9–10 (LIVING BIBLE)

Moses' story is a reminder that God can create the most beautiful outcomes from the hardest beginnings. His mother hid him, then placed him in a basket on the Nile—trusting God with his life. Pharaoh's daughter found and adopted him, and—through God's providence—Moses' own mother was paid to nurse her child.

It doesn't get any better than that!

Some of you have reached a point in life where you look around and say, "Wow, it doesn't get any better than this."

- Your spouse
- Your friends
- That amazing job
- Your car

After all you've endured, you realize you couldn't have orchestrated it better yourself.

When my mother passed, none of her nine siblings wanted me. That might sound sad, but looking back, I see God's hand. My adoptive family raised me in church, poured godly values into me, and gave me what I needed most. My own plan couldn't have worked out better than God's.

Yes, I've had losses.

Yes, I've experienced pain and heartbreak.

But Romans 8:28 says, *All things work together for the good to them that love God, to them who are the called according to His purpose.*

Not just some things—all things.

I am "the called." I am chosen, a royal priesthood called out of darkness into His marvelous light. My mother can rest easy—God had a plan for me before I was born. Even when I didn't understand the tragedy, even when it looked hopeless or I felt abandoned, God was working.

> *"For I know the plans I have for you," declares the Lord,*
> *"plans to prosper you and not to harm you, plans to*
> *give you hope and a future."*
>
> — JEREMIAH 29:11

He created me—He knows what's best for me!

> *You know what I am going to say even before I say it,*
> *LORD.*
>
> — PSALM 139:4

Why do we sometimes think we know better than God? We try to take control, rush the process, or fix things ourselves—only to make a mess. We've all been there. Sometimes, when God seems slow, we try to "help" Him out, but faith means letting God orchestrate the outcome.

> *Without faith it is impossible to please Him, for he who comes to God must believe that He is and that He is a rewarder of those who diligently seek Him.*

> — HEBREWS 11:6

The greatest outcomes come from trusting God.

- Your knowledge isn't enough.
- Your plans aren't enough.
- Your life is nothing without Him.

Sometimes, what looks like a setback is actually God setting you up for something better. Like Job, you may not understand why you're going through, but God is working behind the scenes.

> *All the days of my appointed time will I wait, till my change come.*

> — JOB 14:14

When Job received double for his trouble, I can hear him saying, "It doesn't get any better than this!"

When you've been on the enemy's side, but now you're reaping the benefits of God's favor—doors opening, prayers answered—it really doesn't get any better than this.

A God I can lean and depend on.

A God I can trust.

A God full of grace and mercy.

A God who wakes me up clothed in my right mind.

A God who makes a way out of no way.

A God who does the impossible!

I remember working at the group home, managing three flights of stairs and up to 24 defiant girls at once—fights, chaos, just mess! When I was asked to move to a different unit, I thought it would be even worse. But I had prayed for a place without stairs. God answered —no stairs, manageable girls, and a team that brought so much structure the program ran itself. It didn't even feel like work.

It doesn't get any better than this.

If I'd kept thinking to myself, I would've missed my blessing.

"For my thoughts are not your thoughts, neither are your
ways my ways," declares the Lord.

— ISAIAH 55:8

God will turn your gloom into glamour, your tests into testimonies, your problems into praise, your hurt into hallelujah.

Serving God pays off—and it doesn't get any better than this.

No one can love me like He can.

No one can heal me.

No one can give me peace like Him.

And the peace of God, which passes all understanding, shall
keep your hearts and minds through Christ Jesus.

— PHILIPPIANS 4:7

O taste and see that the Lord is good, and His mercy
endures forever

— PSALM 34:8

Cast your cares upon the Lord, for He cares for you

— 1 PETER 5:7

*Yea, though I walk through the valley of the shadow of
death, I will fear no evil, for Thou art with me*

— PSALM 23:4

CHAPTER 13
I MEAN IT THIS TIME

Acts 9:1–9, 21–22

Before his transformation, Saul (later Paul) was a terror to the early church. He approved of Stephen's murder and made havoc of the church—dragging believers from their homes, committing them to prison, and doing everything in his power to crush the movement of Jesus Christ.

> *"Paul then made havoc of the church, entering every house, and dragging off men and women, committing them to prison."*
>
> — ACTS 8:3

But Saul's story didn't end there. After his encounter with Jesus on the road to Damascus, he was no longer the same man. Sometimes people won't take your transformation seriously until you change your name—and Saul became Paul. He left behind the reputation, the baggage, and the self-protection of his old life.

I get it. Back in the day, I had a name too—Peaches. Peaches was tough, ready to fight, and would protect herself at any cost. But to walk in your calling, you have to let go of the old name, the old ways, and the old wounds. You have to mean it this time.

After Saul's transformation, I imagine him saying, "God, I mean it this time! I'll serve You and You only."

I had my own "Damascus road" moment while working in Germany. God showed me a glimpse of my future and gave me Isaiah 43:1:

> "But now thus saith the Lord that created thee, O
> Jacob... Fear not: for I have redeemed thee, I have
> called thee by thy name; thou art mine."

I knew that if I accepted God's call, I had to mean it. No more playing. No more going back to old habits. I had to surrender my will, my hurts, my disappointments, and let God be God.

We've all made New Year's resolutions and promises to change, only to slip back into old patterns by March. But real change takes a made-up mind: "God, I mean it this time."

We want God's blessings, we want Him to come to our rescue, but are we willing to sell out for Him?

> *"What then? Shall we sin because we are not under law but*
> *under grace? God forbid."*

> — ROMANS 6:15

Sin isn't just murder—

- Unforgiveness
- Gossip
- Lying
- Adultery
- Slander

We defend and minimize these, but God calls us to transformation.

> *Be not conformed to this world, but be transformed by the*
> *renewing of your mind...*

> — ROMANS 12:2

When you're renewed, you want to do things differently. You start praying:

- "God, I want to be acceptable in Your sight!"
- "God, I want to make it in!"
- "God, I don't want to hear, 'Depart from me.'"

Saul left his old life behind—even changed his name. Sometimes you have to change your friends, your habits, your mindset.

> *Let this mind be in you which was also in Christ Jesus...*
> *That you may be blameless and harmless, shining as lights*
> *in the world.*

> — PHILIPPIANS 2:5, 15

My husband says, "I have to live with myself, and I don't want to go to the setting sun and hate myself for the things I've done."
You've got to mean it this time!
It's crucial. It's urgent. It's a downright emergency!

> *No one knows the day or hour... only the Father.*

> — MATTHEW 24:36

Make up your mind to be clean, even if you have to pray Psalm 51:10 every day:

"Create in me a clean heart, O God; and renew a right spirit within me."

God, I mean it this time! You died for me, so I will live for You. What's more important—your feelings or making it in? Who's more important—your friends or making it in? Don't settle for a form of godliness.

Having a form of godliness, but denying the power thereof: from such turn away.

— 2 TIMOTHY 3:5

Don't just talk the talk—walk the walk.

- Don't be one thing at church and another on Facebook.
- Don't sing on Sunday and gossip on Monday.
- Don't pray and then speak filth.

Walk away from what's holding you back—and mean it.

If my people, which are called by my name, shall humble themselves, and pray, and seek my face, and turn from their wicked ways; then will I hear from heaven, and will forgive their sin, and will heal their land.

— 2 CHRONICLES 7:14

God wants to heal you. He wants to deliver you. He's waiting on you.

Now unto Him that is able to keep you from falling...

— JUDE 24

*If we confess our sins, He is faithful and just to forgive us
our sins and to cleanse us from all unrighteousness.*

— 1 JOHN 1:9

*The Lord is not slack concerning His promise... but is
longsuffering, not willing that any should perish but
that all should come to repentance.*

— 2 PETER 3:9

The time is now to grab hold of faith—

- Lord, order my steps.
- Let the words of my mouth and the meditation of my
  heart be acceptable in Your sight, O Lord, my strength and
  my redeemer (Psalm 19:14).

*For God so loved the world that He gave His only begotten
Son...*

— JOHN 3:16

Stop and tell God, "I need You—and I mean it this time!"

CHAPTER 14

A CASE OF THE "I CAN'T HELP ITS!"

I will bless the LORD at all times; His praise shall continually be in my mouth. My soul shall make her boast in the LORD; the humble shall hear thereof and be glad.

— PSALM 34:1

David's words are a pledge: no matter what, I will thank God. Good days or bad—His praise will always be on my lips. It's a declaration of unwavering gratitude and trust, a belief that God is always worthy of our worship.

Sometimes, you just can't help yourself—you have to praise Him.

The "I can't help its" means you're so full of God's goodness, you can't hold back your worship. You're compelled to glorify Him, no matter what others do or say. It's in your blood! Jesus didn't hesitate to die for me, so I won't hesitate to live for Him. I can't help it—it's who I am!

I'm leaning on the Lord's side. It doesn't matter what the crowd is doing—bars, clubs, swearing, or chasing trends. My heart is fixed and focused on Christ. My mind is made up.

My heart is steadfast; I will sing and give praise, even with
my glory.

— PSALM 108:1

A steadfast heart means you're anchored, unwavering, and determined to stick with God even in hard times. Worship is your response to His faithfulness and love.

The song says, "You're the center of my joy!" (Richard Smallwood). That's how I feel—He's the heart of my contentment, the hope for all I do.

I'm about to burst with song; I can't keep quiet about you.

— PSALM 30:12 (MSG)

When your heart is overflowing, praise just bursts out. It's a joy you can't contain and a testimony you can't keep to yourself. This is the kind of "gossip" the world needs—sharing the Good News of Jesus!

By Him therefore let us offer the sacrifice of praise to God
continually, that is, the fruit of our lips giving thanks to
His name.

— HEBREWS 13:15

Sometimes, praise is a sacrifice. You worship even when you don't feel like it. But God created us to glorify Him—our spirits long to give Him honor. When we worship enough to rise above our emotions, true joy and praise begin to flow.

O give thanks unto the LORD; for He is good: for His mercy
endures forever.

— PSALM 136:1

Giving thanks is foundational to Christian living. It's how we show God our love and gratitude for all He is and all He's done. The Bible is filled with reminders to lift our voices in thanksgiving, no matter our circumstances.

From a young age, I was taught to praise God. I remember walking to choir rehearsal with Kesha and Jacy—no one had to make us go, we just wanted to be there. Our friendships were built in the church, and that made it even sweeter. When you start children out early in the church, they "can't help but go" when they're older. Church was all I knew as a child, and now as an adult, I can't help it!

I sang in the choir, served as a junior nurse, ushered, was Sunday school secretary—you name it! When you're a PK (Pastor's Kid), you learn to do it all, and I enjoyed every bit.

The "I can't help its!" is a holy compulsion—a deep, irrepressible drive to worship, serve, and love God.

- My heart is fixed.
- My mind is made up.
- I can't help but praise Him!

CHAPTER 15

"WHAT'S IN YOU WILL COME OUT OF YOU"

He went on: "What comes out of a person is what defiles
them. For it is from within, out of a person's heart, that
evil thoughts come—sexual immorality, theft, murder,
adultery, greed, malice, deceit, lewdness, envy, slander,
arrogance and folly. All these evils come from inside and
defile a person."

— MARK 7:20–23

Anger and frustration are normal emotions—even for Christians. God gave us feelings, but how we respond to them is the real test. How do you react when you're mistreated or misunderstood? With love, patience, and kind words—or with rage and a desire to get even?

The way we respond to life's unexpected challenges and temptations is a clear indicator of whether we're living under the guidance of the Holy Spirit. Spiritual maturity is revealed in how we handle difficult, unpleasant situations that come out of nowhere.

I know what it's like to be short and snappy with people when my heart is hurting. Sometimes, when you're upset, you want to withdraw from everyone. Isolation isn't always bad, but we must give our pain to God and let Him help us process it in a Christ-like way.

Is it possible to suppress anger and frustration and still respond with grace? Yes—if Jesus is truly embedded in our hearts, His character will come out in our actions.

That's why it's so important to pray and fill ourselves with God's Word.

What you take in is what will come out.

Remember when you were a child and swallowed a bead or a coin? It eventually comes out—what goes in will come out!

> *Thy word have I hid in mine heart, that I might not sin*
> *against thee.*
>
> — PSALM 119:11

What's in your heart will show up in your actions.

> *Above all else, guard your heart, for everything you do*
> *flows from it.*
>
> — PROVERBS 4:23

If you don't let God heal your heart, you'll react negatively to everything. Trust will be hard, and it will damage your relationships.

> *But those things which proceed out of the mouth come forth*
> *from the heart, and they defile the man.*
>
> — MATTHEW 15:18

No one wants to be around someone with a nasty attitude. If every word is negative and every interaction is harsh, people will pull away—and you'll be miserable.

The heart is deceitful above all things, and desperately sick;
who can understand it?

— JEREMIAH 17:9

The principle is simple: "Garbage in, garbage out." If you fill your heart with negativity, bitterness, or sin, that's what will come out. But if you fill your heart with God's Word, gratitude, and love, that's what will overflow.

CHAPTER 16
BUT IN THE MEANTIME

Wait for the Lord; be strong and let your heart take courage;
wait for the Lord!

— PSALM 27:14

There are seasons when it feels like God can't see us, can't hear us, or has stopped responding to our prayers. But even in those moments, we can trust that He is with us and in control. Waiting on God is not wasted time—it's a season of expectancy. He will fulfill His promises. He will come through. Even when we can't see Him, He's working behind the scenes on our behalf.

Waiting is hard—especially when you're in a tough place. I remember working jobs that kept me away from church. Sundays, Bible studies, even noonday prayer were off limits because of my schedule. I started praying, "God, give me more time for ministry." Eventually, He answered. I got my dream job at the courthouse, with hours that let me attend every service and prayer meeting. But my hours—and my paycheck—were cut in half. What do you do in the meantime, when your provision doesn't look like your promise? You wait. You trust that because your desire is to serve God, He will supply your needs.

> *But my God shall supply all your need according to His riches in glory by Christ Jesus.*
>
> — PHILIPPIANS 4:19

According to HIS riches—not ours. In the meantime, watch God work. Don't let anyone or anything distract you.

- Stay focused
- Keep your eyes forward
- Don't let the enemy get you off track

The Bible is full of encouragement to wait on the Lord:

> *"Wait on the LORD: Be of good courage, and He shall strengthen thine heart"*
>
> — PSALM 27:14

God promises to give us strength and courage in the waiting. I know it's easier said than done, but I'm living it. I won't write anything in this book that hasn't hit home for me first. I'm encouraging you—hold on and rest in God's promises.

Sarah's story is a powerful reminder. Despite her old age and years of waiting, she held onto faith and saw God's promise fulfilled in the birth of Isaac. Her journey shows us the power of trusting God's timing—even when it doesn't make sense.

Praise Him in the meantime!

- Don't get weary
- Don't get restless
- Don't try to make things happen on your own

Wait like you know it's on the way

WHAT DOES "MEANTIME" MEAN?

It means, "for the moment." But in the Bible, even a moment can have eternal significance.

> *To everything there is a season, and a time for every*
> *purpose under heaven.*

> — ECCLESIASTES 3:1

It won't always be like this. God will turn it around in your favor. You may never know the reason for your wait, but you can trust there IS a reason. Waiting on the Lord means trusting Him, seeking Him, and staying faithful—even when you don't see results yet.

What will you do in the meantime?
How will you act in the meantime?
What will you speak in the meantime?

David's desire was to be with the Lord, to worship Him, and to seek His presence:

> *"One thing I ask from the LORD, this only do I seek: that I*
> *may dwell in the house of the LORD all the days of my*
> *life, to gaze on the beauty of the LORD and to seek Him*
> *in His temple"*

> — PSALM 27:4

CHAPTER 17
CHECK YOUR OIL

The Lord is my shepherd; I shall not want.
He maketh me to lie down in green pastures: he leadeth me
beside the still waters.
He restoreth my soul...
Thou anointest my head with oil; my cup runneth over...
Surely goodness and mercy shall follow me all the days of
my life: and I will dwell in the house of the Lord forever.

— PSALM 23

Oil in scripture is a powerful symbol—God's blessing, His presence, and the power of the Holy Spirit. The overflowing cup and anointing in Psalm 23 remind us: even in the midst of difficulty, God marks, sustains, and honors His people.

Throughout the Bible, oil is used for anointing, for healing, and for setting apart leaders. It represents divine direction, joy, and a supernatural connection to God. When someone "has the oil," it means they're anointed—set apart by God, moving under the power of the Holy Ghost. They don't just sing, dance, or preach; they shift the atmosphere. But here's the truth: everyone must go through their own pressing and shaking to get their own oil. It's personal.

I see it in my children—Yonna, Rey, Diamond, and Javier.

- **Yonna** is a worshipper, using her gifts to reach God's heart. Her "yes" in worship sweeps through a room, marked by obedience and a pure heart.
- **Rey** is a multifaceted drummer, anointed from a young age, his gift overflowing and blessing every service.
- **Diamond** is a devotee of God's song, able to create melodies out of anything. She's a front-line warrior, breaking barriers and saying "yes" to God.
- **Javier** is a worshipper and psalmist, a lover of the Word, diligent in his preparation, a bonafide teaching disciple throughout his song.

Each one carries their own oil, their own mantle, their own unique anointing.

In the natural, oil maintenance is crucial for a healthy engine. Spiritually, it's no different. Here's how to "check your oil" and keep your anointing fresh:

- **Change your oil:**

Regular prayer is essential. Daily, intentional prayer—including praying in the Spirit—keeps you spiritually energized and aware.

- **Don't use the wrong oil:**

Compromise and lack of holiness make room for the enemy. Stay clear of distractions and anything that pulls you away from God.

Revelation 2:4–5 urges believers to return to their first love and the practices that keep them close to Christ.

- **Fill your oil:**

Spend time in the Word. Meditate on scripture. This not only reveals God's will but strengthens your faith and "activates" the oil in your life.

Make these disciplines a daily habit and you'll sustain the anointing, continually experiencing God's power and presence.

Check your oil—don't let your lamp run dry!

CHAPTER 18

YOU SEE THE GLORY,
BUT YOU DON'T
KNOW THE STORY

*But about midnight, when Paul and Silas were praying and
singing hymns of praise to God, and the prisoners were
listening to them; suddenly there was a great
earthquake, so powerful that the very foundations of
the prison were shaken. At once all the doors were
opened and everyone's chains were unfastened. When
the jailer, shaken out of sleep, saw the prison doors
open, he drew his sword and was about to kill himself,
thinking the prisoners had escaped. But Paul shouted,
"Do not hurt yourself, we are all here!"*

— ACTS 16:25–28

We love to celebrate the "glory" moments—the miraculous midnight deliverance, the chains falling off, the victory shout. But so often, we don't know the story behind the glory.

THE BACKSTORY:

Acts 16 opens with Paul and Silas on Paul's second missionary journey. They reach Philippi, where Lydia and her household are converted. As the church grows, Paul casts a demon out of a slave girl, angering her owners who can no longer profit from her. Paul and Silas are dragged before the authorities, falsely accused, beaten, and thrown into jail.

We hear the sermons: "Oh, but at midnight!" But few talk about the pain, the injustice, the struggle, and the faith it took to praise God in the dark—before the earthquake, before the breakthrough.

MINISTRY'S HIDDEN STORY:

People often see the First Lady's hats, the celebrations, the anniversaries—the "glory." But they don't see the internal conflicts, the exhaustion, the heartbreak, the unseen sacrifices. As a First Lady and Bishop's wife, I know what it means to be stretched thin, to carry burdens no one else sees, to pour out for others while quietly tending your own wounds.

I watched my adopted mother, Alean Porter, endure hardships and rejection in ministry with grace. I strive to be at least half the woman she was. What sets me apart is my determination to please God, even when it's hard.

Serving with your spouse in ministry is a privilege, but behind the smiles are moments of heartbreak, fatigue, and unseen struggles. Ministry can sap your spiritual energy and make you feel invisible. But I've learned: having an open, sensitive, and perceptive heart is part of the calling—and God's strength is always enough.

DON'T GET LOST IN THE GLORY—REMEMBER THE STORY:

Paul and Silas didn't enjoy the beatings or the prison cell, but their suffering had a purpose. Their story reminds us: the glory is real, but so is the story behind it. Every testimony of triumph is built on a foundation of faith, perseverance, and unseen battles.

> *But the God of all grace, who hath called us unto his eternal glory by Christ Jesus, after that ye have suffered a while, make you perfect, stablish, strengthen, settle you.*
>
> — 1 PETER 5:10 (KJV)

CHAPTER 19
KEEP THE MAIN THING
THE MAIN THING

*But seek first his kingdom and his righteousness, and all
these things will be given to you as well.*

— MATTHEW 6:33

Life is full of distractions, pressures, and demands. But Jesus calls us to keep our priorities straight—to seek God's kingdom and righteousness above everything else. When we do, everything else falls into place.

*Whatever you do, work at it with all your heart, as
working for the Lord, not for human masters.*

— COLOSSIANS 3:23

This verse reminds us to approach every task with integrity, diligence, and excellence—not just to please people, but to honor God. Your ultimate "boss" is Christ. Your work, no matter how big or small, reflects your relationship with Him. This perspective transforms ordinary tasks into acts of worship and gives your work greater purpose and dignity.

> *Abraham was fully convinced that God is able to do*
> *whatever He promises.*
>
> — ROMANS 4:21

True faith isn't just believing God's promises—it's being absolutely convinced that He will fulfill them, even when circumstances seem impossible. Abraham's faith, rooted in this conviction, was credited to him as righteousness. Even as he and Sarah grew old, he never wavered; he patiently waited, fully persuaded of God's ability to perform.

> *Immediately they left the boat and their father and*
> *followed him.*
>
> — MATTHEW 4:22

James and John dropped everything—family, livelihood, security —to follow Jesus. That's radical commitment. Real discipleship means putting your relationship with Christ first, above all else.

Keeping the main thing the main thing means you're in alignment with God. You're focused on what matters most—your relationship with Him and your spiritual health. When you prioritize God, your life is marked by justice, peace, and joy in the Holy Spirit. You're less distracted, more purposeful, and better equipped to help others and grow closer to God.

Stay focused. Don't let the urgent crowd out the important. Don't let the noise of life drown out God's voice.

- Make time for prayer and the Word.
- Choose faith over fear.
- Say yes to God's call, even when it means letting go of comfort or familiarity.

Keep the main thing the main thing—and watch God handle everything else.

CHAPTER 20
KEEP YOUR BIBLES OPEN

*I have stored up your word in my heart, that I might not
sin against you.*

— PSALM 119:11

Whenever my husband preaches, he always says, "Keep your Bibles open, for I have nothing to offer you outside of the Word of God." That phrase is more than a pulpit habit—it's a way of life.

Scripture tells us the Bible is "living and active," "profitable for teaching," and the very foundation of faith. Reading your Bible isn't just a religious routine; it's the lifeline for your soul.

- It helps you resist sin.
- It equips you for every good work.
- It builds faith, brings peace, and reveals God's heart.

THREE BENEFITS OF READING THE BIBLE DAILY

1. Growth in faith and a deeper relationship with God
2. Wisdom and guidance for life's decisions
3. Courage and peace in the face of challenges

Daily reading grounds you, nourishes your spirit, and gives you hope and perspective for whatever you face.

Remember how Big Mama used to leave the Bible open on the coffee table? Now, some folks don't even own a Bible—or can't find one if they do. But it's the Word that will sustain us, especially in these uncertain times. With so many decisions being made about our lives, and so much out of our control, the Bible is our anchor.

- Without the Word, we become spiritually weak, morally unstable, and confused.
- Ignoring God's Word strains our relationship with Him and leaves us vulnerable to deception and despair.

The Bible reveals God's promises and purposes for our lives. It's the only foundation that will keep, sustain, and guide us. You simply cannot operate outside of the Word!

How can we truly know God and His intentions for our lives without His Word?

- How would we know that Jesus is the only way (John 14:6)?
- How would we know how to live, what truth is, or how to stand in these last days?

Without the Word, we're left with every fantasy of man's heart—no absolutes, no truth, only confusion. We'd be absolutely lost.

We need guidance, direction, and a path of righteousness. Without the Bible, we're tossed about, going every which way. I could go on and on about the significance of God's Word, but the real question is: Do you value it? Are you spending time in it daily?

Sadly, many have multiple Bibles at home but rarely open them. If that's you, why not start today? Read the greatest book ever written —God's personal gift to you. Let it revitalize your relationship with Jesus.

Disregarding God's Word has far-reaching, negative effects on every area of life. But following it brings wisdom, protection, and blessing.

Keep your Bible open—keep your heart open—and let the Word of God transform your life.

CHAPTER 21
YOU DID HEAR HIM

The Lord called Samuel: and he answered, "Here am I."
Three times Samuel heard the call, and three times he
ran to Eli, thinking it was the priest calling him.
Finally, Eli realized it was God, and told Samuel: "If He
calls you again, say, 'Speak, Lord, for your servant
hears.'"

— 1 SAMUEL 3:2–9

Do you remember when the Lord first called your name?
Maybe it was in a church pew, at your kitchen sink, or driving down the street. You heard that small, still voice calling you out—"It's your time!"

God's call is unmistakable, but sometimes we confuse it for something else. Like Samuel, you might be looking for confirmation, wondering, "Did I really hear Him?" Yes—you DID hear Him!

> *"Listen carefully. I'm getting ready to do something in Israel*
> *that is going to shake everyone up and get their*
> *attention!"*

> — 1 SAMUEL 3:11 (MSG)

God is about to open doors for you, but you have to be in position to hear Him. Don't mistake His voice for another, and don't let anything keep you from answering His call.

You have a mandate.

You have work to do.

You have a call on your life for such a time as this.

Nothing is more important than answering God's call. There's nothing you're in that He won't forgive or turn around. Don't lose your destiny by ignoring His voice.

If God called you, He's already equipped you for what's now and what's to come.

> *May God equip you with everything good for doing His*
> *will, and may He work in us what is pleasing to Him,*
> *through Jesus Christ.*

> — HEBREWS 13:21

It's not always easy, but God's got you!

> *Before I formed you in the womb, I knew you; before you*
> *were born, I sanctified you; I ordained you a prophet to*
> *the nations.*

> — JEREMIAH 1:5

He already had your assignment planned. Your job is to walk in it. Pray and ask God what your assignment is. Are you serving in the right area? Are you effective and passionate about it? Don't just serve —serve in your calling!

- Get on board.
- Stand on business.
- Walk the walk, not just talk the talk.

He didn't make a mistake. You DID hear Him.

You might ask, "Me? Did He really mean to call me?" Yes—He did! And you heard Him.

When I called my kids, I wouldn't tell them what I wanted until they came to me. I wanted them to see my face and not misunderstand the assignment. God calls you directly, without distractions, so you won't get talked out of your purpose.

Get to the point where you say:

- "God, I'll trust You."
- "God, I'll obey You."
- "Even though I walk through the valley, I will not fear."
- "Though He slay me, yet will I trust Him."

If God is for us, who can be against us?

— ROMANS 8:31

I can do all things through Christ who gives me strength.

— PHILIPPIANS 4:13

God has not given us a spirit of fear, but of power, love, and a sound mind.

— 2 TIMOTHY 1:7

"The Lord is my helper; I will not be afraid. What can man do to me?"

— HEBREWS 13:6

If God is for you, He's more than the whole world against you. God called us. We've got this!

CHAPTER 22
I WILL GO!

> *But Ruth replied, "Don't urge me to leave you or to turn*
> *back from you. Where you go, I will go, and where you*
> *stay I will stay. Your people will be my people and your*
> *God my God."*

— RUTH 1:16

Ruth's words to Naomi are a powerful declaration of loyalty, faith, and willingness to step into the unknown. Sometimes, to be blessed and to be a blessing, you have to uproot yourself from what's comfortable and familiar.

Don't hesitate.

Don't stall.

Don't say, "I'll have to pray about it."

Don't ask a friend for advice when God is nudging you—just do it!

Saying "yes" to God isn't always easy, but it's always worth it. For your sake, God, I will go.

> *Then I heard the voice of the Lord saying, "Whom shall I*
> *send? And who will go for us?" And I said, "Here am I.*
> *Send me!"*

— ISAIAH 6:8

Isaiah saw the Lord, recognized his own unworthiness, and still answered God's call: "Send me." That's what it means to be a servant —ready to go, ready to obey, ready to trust.

I will go!
I will do Your will.
It's my duty.
It's my obligation.

Sometimes you have to pray, "Order my steps," and be ready to move when God says move.

Throughout scripture, when God called, His people responded:

- Moses led the Israelites out of Egypt (Exodus 3:7–10).
- Jonah was sent to Nineveh—eventually he obeyed, and the city repented (Jonah 3:1–2).
- Abraham was told to take Isaac to Moriah and offer him to God (Genesis 22:1–2).

Obedience is key.

Stop questioning God—just go!

But you must know His voice.

Let's be honest: sometimes, as soon as we hear there's "extra church," we've already decided, "Oh, I'm not going!" We nod in agreement, but our minds are made up. We miss blessings because of disobedience. God knows what's best—trust the process. It's not always easy, attractive, or comfortable, but it all works together for our good.

Church is where we need to be!

- It's where we get instruction.
- It's where we gain clarity and understanding.
- Yes, we can read our Bibles at home, but church is where the Word comes alive and we grow together.

There's no sacrifice in just "watching the live." God honors obedience and faith in action.

When a Christian says, "I'll go," it's a leap of faith—accepting God's instructions and stepping into His purpose, even when the details are unclear. Sometimes it's a specific place, sometimes it's a new mission, sometimes it's just a willingness to serve wherever He leads.

Trust God—He won't lead you astray.

You just have to go.

CHAPTER 23

DON'T MISTAKE MODIFICATION FOR TRANSFORMATION

Acts 9:1–12, 17–18

Let's be real: there's a big difference between modification and transformation.

- **Modification** is a change or alteration—just making something work a little better, patching it up, dressing it up, or covering it over.
- **Transformation** is a thorough, dramatic change—a brand new thing, inside and out.

A lot of people settle for religious modification instead of true spiritual transformation.

> *Therefore, if anyone is in Christ, he is a new creature: old things are passed away; behold, all things have become new.*

> — 2 CORINTHIANS 5:17

When you're transformed, your thinking is new, your mindset is new, and your life is new. When you're just modified, you're only dressing up the old—you're still the same on the inside.

- Modification means: "I stopped doing envious things."
- Transformation means: "I'm no longer envious, even in my heart."
- Modification means: "I stopped talking about you."
- Transformation means: "I can celebrate you, even if we've had a falling out."

Sometimes we fool others—and ourselves—by pretending we've changed, when all we've done is modify our behavior. But transformation is deeper:

- Modification covers up pain.
- Transformation gives pain to God and lets Him deliver you.
- Modification keeps people at a distance.
- Transformation welcomes them with love.
- Modification says, "I'll feed you with a long-handled spoon."
- Transformation says, "I'll invite you to dinner—and pay for it."

PAUL'S STORY:

Before his conversion, Saul was a Pharisee who persecuted the church. On the road to Damascus, he was blinded by a light and heard Jesus' voice. That encounter didn't just modify Saul—it transformed him. He became Paul, a new man with a new mission.

Paul's story shows that God doesn't just want to patch us up—He wants to make us brand new. God can use unlikely people for His undeniable plan!

TELL YOURSELF: I'M NOT MODIFIED—I'M TRANSFORMED!

I think about when my husband drives my car and hits every bump and pothole. I tell him (nicely) that if he breaks it, I want it fixed—not patched, but made brand new. Some of us are patching up things in our lives that need to be made new—our hearts, our minds, our habits.

- Out with the old, in with the new.
- I'm no longer that old person.
- **Transformed, not modified!**

You can't keep doing the old things, talking the old talk, and claim transformation.

No one puts new wine into old wineskins... the new wine
will burst the wineskins and be spilled...

— MATTHEW 9:17

You can't force God's new thing into your old ways. God is trying to do something new, but you keep holding onto the old.

Before I formed you in the womb, I knew you; before you
were born, I set you apart.

— JEREMIAH 1:5

God is looking for butterflies—you keep settling for being a caterpillar. Don't crawl when you can soar!

Stop putting a band-aid on it; let God heal it. Stop questioning; trust God to turn it all around.

- Modification says, "I'm okay."
- Transformation runs to the altar and lets God have it.
- Modification says, "I've got this."
- Transformation says, "God, I cast all my cares on You."
- Modification tries to fix it.
- Transformation trusts the Lord with all your heart.
- Modification comes up with a plan.
- Transformation says, "Even though I walk through the valley, I will fear no evil—for You are with me."

CHAPTER 24
DON'T MISS IT

*"Look, I am coming soon! My reward is with me, and I will
give to each person according to what they have done."*

— JOHN 14:3

Some time ago, I had what you might call "just a dream," but to me, it was a nightmare. I dreamt I was at church, part of a lineup of speakers. Someone came to my dressing room and said, "Lady Baker, you're next"—but I wasn't dressed, my hair wasn't done, I wasn't ready. The person before me was almost finished, and I was nowhere near prepared. I believe God was warning me: don't let anything or anyone make you miss your moment! What if the Lord called your name right now? Would you be ready?

*"But of that day and hour knoweth no man, no, not the
angels of heaven, but my Father only."*

— MATTHEW 24:36

You won't have time to get ready. You've got to stay ready. That dream shook me—I started searching myself, asking the Lord, "Where am I lacking? What am I doing? Lord, don't let me be caught with my work undone."

"Now finish the work, so that your eager willingness to do it
may be matched by your completion of it..."

— 2 CORINTHIANS 8:11

Let your start match your finish. Let your words match your deeds. Don't miss it!

"You ran well. Who hindered you from obeying the truth?"

— GALATIANS 5:7

Who or what is so important that you'd risk missing God's call? You started off strong—praying, fasting, reading the Word, attending church—and now you're making excuses. Where did you fall off? What got in the way?

This is not the time to take a break or fall out. This is urgent!

You have a number, and it will be called. Are you ready?

"Christ has put each part of the church in its right place.
Each part helps other parts...This is what is needed to
keep the whole body together...the whole body grows
strong in love."

— EPHESIANS 4:16 (NLV)

It takes all of us. Yes, it's hard—but the way of transgressors is harder.

> *"Good understanding giveth favour: but the way of*
> *transgressors is hard."*

— PROVERBS 13:15

If you're living unfaithful, deceiving, disloyal, or hypocritical, of course it's hard!

A hypocrite is someone who claims to believe one thing but lives another.

> *"You will know them by their fruits."*

— MATTHEW 7:16

People should know who you belong to by how you live.

> *"Don't you know that when you offer yourselves to someone*
> *as obedient slaves, you are slaves to the one you obey...?"*

— ROMANS 6:16

Don't become a slave to anything or anyone but God. Don't let anything separate you from Him!

> *"Who shall separate us from the love of Christ? Shall*
> *tribulation, or distress, or persecution, or famine, or*
> *nakedness, or peril, or sword?"*

— ROMANS 8:35

Nothing!

> *"For what shall it profit a man, if he shall gain the whole world, and lose his own soul? Or what shall a man give in exchange for his soul?"*

> — MARK 8:36-37

Don't miss heaven trying to please your flesh here on earth. Nothing is worth missing church, missing your assignment, missing your soul's salvation. Make sacrifices—your time, your comfort, your resources. Christ made the ultimate sacrifice for us while we were yet sinners.

> *"But God commendeth his love toward us, in that, while we were yet sinners, Christ died for us."*

> — ROMANS 5:8

It's not enough to talk about it—your actions must line up.

You won't come back to service for just an hour and fifteen minutes?

> *"Not forsaking the assembling of ourselves together, as the manner of some is; but exhorting one another: and so much the more, as ye see the day approaching."*

> — HEBREWS 10:25

Time is short. Be sold out. Don't miss it!

Don't let the enemy trick you.

- It's not the time to fall out.
- It's not the time to throw in the towel.
- It's not the time to give up.

Hold to God's unchanging hand.

Let Him order your steps.

Look to the hills from which comes your help—your help comes from the Lord.

Greater is He that is in you than he that is in the world.

Yea, though you walk through the valley, He is with you.

Lift up your heads, O ye gates—let your light shine.

Don't miss it!

CHAPTER 25

SOMETIMES YOU
JUST GOTTA HOLLA!

*In my affliction I called upon the Lord, and I cried to my
God: And he heard my voice from his holy temple: and
my cry before him came into his ears. The earth shook
and trembled: the foundations of the mountains were
troubled and were moved, because he was angry with
them.*

— PSALM 18:6–7 (DRB)

Sometimes life gets so heavy, so overwhelming, that you can't just whisper a prayer—you've got to holla!

There are moments when you have to call out to God from the depths of your soul, because you know nobody else can rescue you. Some things are too big for you, but never too big for God.

BARTIMAEUS IN JERICHO

Bartimaeus, a blind beggar, sat beside the road and heard Jesus was passing by. He cried out, "Jesus, Son of David, have mercy on me!" When people tried to silence him, he shouted even louder. That's faith in action—he refused to let anyone or anything keep him from his breakthrough. When Jesus asked what he wanted, Bartimaeus boldly replied, "Please grant that I recover my sight." Jesus said, "Go your way; your faith has made you well." Instantly, Bartimaeus received his sight and followed Jesus, praising God.

Sometimes, you've got to get loud with your need—call out to God and make your request known.

- Holla when you're desperate.
- Holla when you're in trouble.
- Holla because you know God is the only one who can turn it around.

God offers comfort, courage, and direction in our darkest times. The Bible is full of reminders that we are never alone—God is always with us, supporting and sustaining us through every challenge. Think of Abraham and Isaac, who faced the impossible and found deliverance through faith. Trusting God in the hard places will always reveal His faithfulness.

IMPOSSIBLE SITUATIONS

When I say "an impossible situation," I mean those obstacles that feel like they have no solution. Maybe you've gotten bad news from the doctor, maybe your workplace is toxic, maybe you're longing for companionship or a breakthrough that seems out of reach. Whatever it is, God has a reason for every hardship you face. He's working behind the scenes, even when you can't see it.

People may fail you. Friends may turn their backs. But God never fails. He is there every step, every year, every moment you call out for help.

PERSONAL TESTIMONY

Every November, I grieve the birthdays of my birth mother and my first daughter—both now with the Lord. Every year, I say, "This time I'll celebrate their lives," but the pain still comes. Erica lived only a month; my mother died when I was almost three. It's a sadness that could swallow me whole—but God's comfort, peace, and love have carried me through every season.

His mercies keep us from being consumed. He is faithful, and He won't let the enemy oppress us forever.

Sometimes you just gotta holla! God hears you. He's moved by your cry. And He will answer.

THE CONCLUSION

Dear reader, as I bring this book to a close, know that every chapter was written from a place of intentional transparency. These pages are a testament to how important God is to me. Each message spoke to me first—helping me make it through hard times, encouraging myself, and now, I pray, encouraging you.

These are godly principles straight from heaven. When you have nothing left, you can turn to God. When hope feels lost, you can call on the name of Jesus. When you're at your end, that's when God is ready to take control.

Maybe you're in the right place right now for a miracle. Don't give up—stay in the race and keep your eyes on the prize. My hope is to encourage you, just as others have encouraged me, by sharing God's word with life lessons and simple, practical understanding.

I do my best to live God's word and keep His commandments. What you see in these pages is a real journey—not always easy, but absolutely possible and worth it.

Through my writing, imagine me reaching out with a firm handshake and saying: Hello, my name is Daphanny C. Baker, and I offer you Christ today. I offer you a way out—and a way in to God's plan for your life. Jesus is the way, the truth, and the life. Will you accept Him into your heart today?

One thing I love most about writing is the chance to be translucent—to tell my story, to set the stage for the one true and living God. Writing is everything to me—this is my fifth book. When I go through tough times, I don't just go through in silence; I speak out, so others know you can make it, too. There is hope in the storm. There is someone you can grab hold of when it feels like the bottom has fallen out. There's no way to live this life without the word of God lighting your path. No matter how windy or bumpy the road, you'll find God is right there with you.

In the midst of chaos, I keep scriptures close:

- **Job 14:14:** "All the days of my appointed time will I wait, till my change come."
- **Psalm 23:5:** "He's preparing a table before me in the presence of my enemies."
- **Romans 8:37:** "Despite all these things, overwhelming victory is ours through Christ, who loved us."

You can make it. You can get through this. You can come out unscathed because God's Word says He'll never leave you nor forsake you (Hebrews 13:5).

Remember:

You're a champion—even if you don't get a standing ovation.

You're a winner—even if no one gives you a medal.

There is an eternal reward for all who believe.

And as I live my life, this scripture is my prayer and my anchor:

> *Let the words of my mouth, and the meditation of my heart, be acceptable in thy sight, O LORD, my strength, and my redeemer.*

> — PSALM 19:14

Thank you for letting me share this journey with you. May God keep you, strengthen you, and lead you all the way home.

AFTERWORD

Every fourth Sunday, I eagerly anticipate the powerful message God delivers through Lady Daphanny as she ministers to His people. These pages offer a firsthand glimpse of what it's like to be present when she shares God's word with conviction and clarity.

This book is a testament to the profound wisdom God has placed within her, paired with her unmistakable call-to-action approach. The messages here do more than enlighten—they invite you to reflect deeply on your own faith journey, the choices you've made, and those still ahead.

For many years, I've been privileged to witness her share knowledge and inspiration with countless individuals she's been chosen to serve. Now, you have the opportunity to receive this insight for yourself. Lady Daphanny is wholeheartedly devoted to the Lord and takes her divine assignment seriously. She is not only an anointed vessel, but also a messenger appointed by God to spread His word far and wide.

Best,

— JAVIER A. VALENTIN - HER SON

ABOUT THE AUTHOR

Daphanny Baker is a Victim/Witness Advocate in the District Attorney's Office and an inspirational author, known for works such as 365 Days of Transparency, Lady Daphanny's Altar, The Messenger, Peaches Can Do It, and the forthcoming novel The Messenger 2. Drawing inspiration from life's journey and God's intervention in the lives of His children, Daphanny writes to uplift and encourage readers everywhere.

A Pennsylvania resident, she shares her life with her husband—a Pastor—and their four children. Daphanny holds a B.S. in Criminal Justice, an MBA, and a Master of Divinity. Her diverse career includes serving as an astute corrections officer, supervisor in the juvenile justice system, esteemed Pastor's wife, and Elder in the Lord's Church. Her spiritual journey has taken her across the globe, including Europe, as she continues to walk boldly in her God-given assignment.

facebook.com/daphanny.baker

ALSO BY DAPHANNY C. BAKER

365 Days of Transparency

The Messenger

Lady Daphanny's Altar: My prayer for you today is...

Peaches Can Do It!

www.ingramcontent.com/pod-product-compliance
Lightning Source LLC
Chambersburg PA
CBHW051510050726
47594CB00010B/4042